Old Polmont, Laurieston, Redding and Brightons
John Hood

This early view shows the section of Bo'ness Road, Polmont, known locally as Kirk Brae, near its junction with Smiddy Brae. The single storey cottages on the right were demolished in the 1960s when the road was realigned as part of a programme of road improvements as the M9 was built. These also saw Smiddy Brae being widened and the loss of the cottage at the junction, on the left hand side. The other cottages on the left survive, now separated from the realigned road by a wide verge which includes part of the old road.

© John Hood and Lewis Hutton, 2022
First published in the United Kingdom, 2022,
by Stenlake Publishing Ltd.
www.stenlake.co.uk
ISBN 978-1-84033-911-6

The publishers regret that they cannot supply
copies of any pictures featured in this book.

Printed by
Blissetts, Unit E1-E8 Shield Drive, West Cross Ind Pk, Brentford, TW8 9EX

I would like to dedicate this book to John Hood. While it might seem unusual for a book to be dedicated to its author, unfortunately I have good reason. During the preparation of this book John died. He left copious notes, backed up by extensive research, and it has been my privilege to digest them and write this book. I have retained the content of John's partially written captions as far as possible, stitched together his notes and answered the queries for further research he left himself. It is possible that in so doing I have introduced some errors in which case I apologise.

Lewis Hutton

Further Reading

The following were the principal books and websites used by the author during his research. *Falkirk's Trams and Early Buses* is available from Stenlake Publishing. For any of the other titles please contact your local bookshop, reference library or search for them on the internet.

Bradley, Sylvia et al *Westquarter Memories,* Westquarter and Redding Community Project, 2011.
Brotchie, Alan, *Falkirk's Trams and Early Buses,* 2011.
Currie, James M., *Muiravonside and Shieldhill Parish Church 1864-2014.*
Dickson, John, *Polmont and the Braes,* Falkirk District Libraries, 1992.
Falkirk District Libraries, *Shieldhill – A Glimpse of the Past,* 1987.
Gifford, John & Walker, Frank Arneil, *The Buildings of Scotland: Stirling and Central Scotland,* RIAS, 2002.
Laurieston Reminiscence Group, *Happy Valley: Memories of Laurieston,* undated.
Jaques, Richard, *Falkirk and District: an illustrated architectural guide,* The Rutland Press, 2001.
Leask, David, *A Historic Tour of the Parish of Muiravonside,* 2018.
Leask, David, *Westquarter: the story of an estate, from family estate to model village,* Falkirk Libraries and Museums, 1986.
Reid, John *California and Shieldhill,* Falkirk Local History Society, 2005.
Reid, John *The Place Names of Falkirk and East Stirlingshire,* Falkirk Local History Society, 2009.
Scott Ian, Falkirk Local History Society Walk Number 4 *Beancross-Parkhill-Millfield-Old Polmont,* 2005.
Scott, Ian, Falkirk Local History Society website: *Polmont and Brightons.*

Acknowledgements

The author would like to thank Willie Fleming for all his help. The publisher would like to thank Bill Smith for the use of images.

The Wallacestone Memorial (and adjoining flagpole) seen here around 1903. The 8 feet tall obelisk was erected in August 1810 by the inhabitants of Wallacestone just off the Main Street in the public park. The railings and flagpole were added later and were officially opened on 11th September 1890. The memorial marks the spot where, according to legend, William Wallace placed a stone while he watched the approach of the English army before the Battle of Falkirk in 1298. In the 1840s the memorial was the favoured venue of the Methodist lay preacher, Alexander Patrick, who held open air meetings there until his congregation built him a church beside the burn at the foot of Wallacestone Brae.

Introduction

Polmont

Present day Polmont comprises a number of previously quite separate and independent villages. The original settlement of Polmont (now designated Old Polmont) lay to the north of the present village, on Bo'ness Road near Smiddy Brae.

The construction of the Edinburgh – Stirling Turnpike (now A803 in Polmont) c. 1750 shifted the focus of the village south to its present day location. The beginnings of the present day 'new town' of Polmont (or Bennetstown as it was originally known taking its name from Patrick Bennet the first minister of the parish) dates approximately from the erection of a parish church in 1732.

In 1842 the Edinburgh & Glasgow Railway opened a station half a mile to the south of Main Street. Convenient for Edinburgh, Glasgow and Stirling the village grew and developed another centre clustered around the station.

On 28th August 1968 the first section of the M9 Motorway was opened, between Polmont and Falkirk consolidating Polmont's position as a central place to live. Today many people reside in housing that occupies the grand estates of the former industrialists and use its roads and railway to commute to Glasgow, Edinburgh, and the petrochemical works at Grangemouth.

Laurieston

Laurieston was a planned village. Before Francis Napier 6th Lord Napier started feuing the lands of Langton in 1756, there was just a scatter of cottages and farmhouses. He called the new settlement 'New Merchiston' after the family's seat, Merchiston Castle (which he reacquired in 1752 after the family sold it 1659), and planned a grid of streets around a large market square. He sold the project to Sir Lawrence Dundas, 1st Baronet on 31st December 1762, who in 1765 changed the name to Lawrencetown which after a few years became Laurieston.

Its most famous resident was Alfred Nobel inventor of dynamite, who lived at Hawthorn Cottage on Polmont Road while he established his explosives factories in Scotland. Nobel bought the cottage from George McRoberts of the Westquarter Chemical Company, when George became factory manager at Nobel Enterprises' Ardeer Works, Ayrshire.

Westquarter

Almost 200 years later, in 1934, Westquarter House and Estate were purchased by Stirlingshire County Council for another planned village. A scale model of the 'Model' Village was exhibited at the Empire Exhibition in Bellahouston Park, Glasgow, in 1938, to show that Stirlingshire was a leader in new communities with shops and recreational facilities.

Redding

The village of Redding is one of the older settlements in the area and is shown on Timothy Pont's map of Stirlingshire from c. 1590. Coal was mined in Redding before the Union Canal was opened in 1822. After the canal was built the ease and cost of transporting goods to Edinburgh made the industry boom. Many pits were sunk in the area and abandoned as they were worked out. It was one of these that caused the accident that Redding's name is still associated with today when, in 1923, 40 men died as a result of water from an abandoned mine bursting into the workings of No. 23 pit.

Adjacent to the pit was the Westquarter Chemical Company's works, established 1871, which produced sulphuric acid. The acid was crucial to the nitration process when making nitroglycerine, and the works became part of Nobel Enterprises. The Redding factory made detonators for other explosives. At its peak during the Second World War the plant employed 1,700 people, mostly women. It continued to be an important employer until its closure in 1969.

Shieldhill

Another settlement shown on Pont's map of Stirlingshire as Sheelhill suggesting that it was a sheiling where livestock were grazed on summer pastures. By 1855 there was a row of miner's cottages at Easter Sheildhill as well as clusters of cottages at Herdshill, Greenmount and Crosshall strung along the ridge. Mining continued to be the mainstay of the village's economy.

Brightons

Brightons owes its existence to Brighton Quarry which may have been in operation in the 17th century. Once the Union Canal opened the quarry became a source for the stone used in Edinburgh's New Town and also for several buildings in Falkirk. In 1893 it became the location of Lodge Polmont No. 793 after a petition to establish a local lodge was successful.

Established Church, Polmont.

In this view, are both the replacement church (left) and the ruins of the original Polmont North Parish church then covered in ivy (right). The first Gothic-style parish church (the ruins) was built by mason Adam Howison. The foundation stone was laid on 22nd May 1731 and it opened for worship in 1732. It was T-shaped, rubble walled and had a pulpit on the long wall and three long galleries. According to the minister in 1844 it was 'too small damp, ill-arranged and most inadequate seating only 607 of the 749 strong congregation'. During the ministry of the Rev. John Ker, it was replaced by the new church with the foundation stone laid on 10th May 1844, and opened for worship July 1845. The twin-spires on its eastern front are unusual and the church could seat 900 worshippers. Edinburgh architect John Tait's design is in a simplified Lombardic Romanesque style and was built by local stone mason William Thorburn, using stone quarried at Brightons and Maddiston. Within the church there is a stained glass window gifted in memory of Johan Theodor Salveson of Mandel, Norway, who died at Polmont House on 23rd December 1865. Hung in the south tower is a 15-cwt church bell gifted by the Logan family of Clarkston in 1870. The church has had several changes of name including Polmont North Church (1929) and Polmont Old Church (1977) at which time the Polmont South Church was re-named Brightons Parish Church.

A school was opened almost directly opposite the present day Parish Church by local heritors in 1789 on the site of an older kirk school. Built with square rubble walls, it consisted of two rooms upstairs and downstairs. Another room and a smaller wing were built at a later date. The school was open to boys only. Pupils who required to board did so at the nearby Orchard House. The headmaster, Thomas Girdwood who was also clerk to the heritors, served for over 50 years. The hall, on the left, was considerably altered when it was converted to a house, the old schoolhouse being demolished in the early 1960s.

Polmont Bank Hotel   No. 4336

Polmont Bank House and grounds occupied the land between Main Street and Bo'ness Road extending to a point roughly midway between Greenpark Drive and Marchmont Avenue near the former police station. The house stood near Bo'ness Road on what is now the northern edge of Aldi's car park and was probably built in the late 18th century. It was offered for sale or let on several occasions before finally ending up, about 1924, in the hands of Alexander William Steven, the chairman of Allied Ironfounders who owned the house until his death in 1952. After that the house lay empty for a few years. In 1955 Stirling and Clackmananshire Joint Police Board enquired about building a police station at the entrance to the grounds on Main Street. The house sat empty until the early 1960s when it was redeveloped as a hotel, with a bar and a ten-pin bowling alley. By 1990 it had been cleared to make way for the Co-op who sold their store to Aldi in 2015. The lodge house survives on Main Street.

Looking along Main Street Polmont from the east c. 1905 and with Bo'ness Road to the back of the photographer. To the right of the photograph the high stone wall encloses the policies of Polmont Bank; the stone pillars (by the telegraph pole) mark the entrance to the grounds. The lodge house still has the broken stump of one pillar marking its driveway. On the left hand side of the road the buildings were cleared by the mid-1980s to make way for Oakbank Care Home. The home was closed in 2017 and has now been demolished leaving a gap site where houses will be built. In the distance behind the head of the boy third from the right is the white gable of the Black Bull a lonely survivor in this view today.

Early view looking east from Station Road along Main Street, Polmont. The stone wall on the left is Polmont Bank estate, its entrance is next to the two boys standing on the unpaved road.

In this view, taken in 1928, the photographer is standing at the entrance to Station Road looking west along the Main Street in Polmont. Of the properties seen here on the left only the Black Bull Inn and an adjoining two-storey property called Croftfoot House remain. The two-storey property and the terraced row of single-storey cottages to the east of the inn have been replaced by a fairly modern suite of shops. On the other side of the street Bennett Cottage (the single-storey cottage) remains as does the Parish Church Hall. The two-storey property with twin porches was known as Bennett Place. In addition to the Black Bull Inn, Polmont at one time had three other public houses, namely, the Crown, the Lion and McFalls. The family most associated with the Black Bull Inn were the Cruickshanks who ran it for almost 100 years.

The 'public school' was used for congregational meetings and social events, until finally the congregation resolved to erect a church hall. Initially, the offer of a suitable site by James McKillop MP of Polmont House on the site of the old bowling green on Main Street was accepted, with plans for a main hall accommodating 300 and two side halls. Falkirk architect James Strang was appointed to come up with a design. In early 1898 an offer of an alternative site, adjoining Polmont Library in Back Row, was made by David Mitchell of Millfield House. Although initially accepted by the session, Strang advised that the bowling green site had greater potential for future expansion. On Thursday 11th May 1899, the new hall was officially opened. In 1963 a second hall was added. The two workmen, on Main Street, are perhaps operating a street cleaning/levelling machine and further along the street (in the far distance) is probably a steam engine and more workmen. Behind the photographer, on the south side of Main Street, was Millfield Dairy.

Millfield Dairy, Polmont.

Thomas Campbell, owner of Millfield House, established the dairy at Thornhall Farm in the late 19th century. Its tenant, William Ritchie, ran the dairy until the 1940s. It was sold as Ivybank Dairy in 1943 and at that time had byre space for 35 cows, 64 acres of grazing and daily milk sales of 60 gallons. It was bought by Brown Ferguson who ran it until his death, in 1976. His sons took over, expanded the business, and in 1989 they sold it to Hamilton's of East Kilbride. Two years later the dairy was closed and the land sold for housing. Until then the sight of cows ambling along Main Street to the dairy was a common sight, coming from fields around Marchmont Avenue. In 1991 the Fergusons developed Ivybank House Care Home on the site of their former family home, which they ran until 2007 when they sold it to Meallmore.

MILLFIELD, POLMONT.—Residence of D. Mitchell, Esq.

Millfield House could justifiably claim to be the grandest of the several large mansions in the Polmont area. This reputation was enhanced by its first owner John Miller a civil engineer with the Edinburgh & Glasgow Railway Company who rose to become Secretary of the North British Railway Company. It was said of him that he devoted large amounts of time to enhancing Millfield House by, for example, installing gas lighting throughout the house in 1855 and, later, adding the tall central 'outlook tower' to further enhance his view of the surrounding area. The grounds around the house were likewise improved by the addition in 1852 of a glass conservatory in the style of the Crystal Palace, and the construction of a hydraulic ram to draw water for hosehold use from the Polmont Burn that ran through the grounds. In 1865 Miller sold the house to Thomas Campbell, who owned it for twenty years before it was sequestered when his fortunes failed in 1885. It then passed into the ownership of David Mitchell, who continued to develop the house and grounds. He established a stud farm at the Millfield Dairy, and in 1900 the Glasgow firm of William Moyes & Sons, deemed their contract, to replace the existing oil gas plant servicing Millfield House with a new acetylene plant, sufficiently prestigious to issue this postcard advertising their services. Suffering from ill health, David Mitchell sold the house and dairy (with William Ritchie as tenant) in two lots in 1912. The house was bought by John Stein and remained in the family until 1968 when it was sold to property developers and demolished.

Wilson Avenue was originally part of the Back Row which ran to Marchmont Avenue, until it was truncated in the mid-1960s by the newly-built Station Road. Aside from the block of more modern houses the other properties on the left were demolished shortly afterwards. In the main, the ordinary dwellings were confined to the south side of Main Street and typically comprised a long narrow yard at the back. A further series of properties on what would become the Back Row were built to the south parallel to Main Street, with a third even further south at Gardenhead. The hedges on the right of photograph mark the ends of the gardens belonging to the houses on Main Street. At one time there was a sewing school in the Back Row run by Miss McPherson. Later the building was used as a public library.

Polmont House, seen here around 1908, was built about 1785 for Sir Gilbert Lawrie, an Edinburgh apothecary who rose to become HM's Apothecary and Druggist, a position he held for the rest of his life. He was also a director of the Royal Bank of Scotland and was Lord Provost of Edinburgh in 1766 and 1772. He died at Polmont House on 10th September 1787. The house has since been sold, let and resold many times. In 1841, it was briefly the base of operation while the Polmont section of the Edinburgh and Glasgow Railway was built. Its engineer, John Walker, lived at Polmont House while he waited to move into nearby Parkhill House. In May 1844 the 150 acre Polmont estate, comprising Polmont House together with a farm house and steading on Polmontside Farm, was offered for sale. It was acquired in 1845 so that "an establishment for the board and education of young ladies" run by the Misses Telfer of Edinburgh could be opened in 1846, but this didn't last long. By 1851 the house was back in private ownership, this time by the ship owner, James Smith. Another ship owner, Johan Theodor Salveson, owned it until his death in December 1865 – his company would eventually become Christian Salveson. There is a stained glass window in the Old Parish Church dedicated to his memory. In 1880, Polmont House was offered for let, when it comprised three public rooms, seven bedrooms, two dressing rooms and simple servants' and kitchen accommodation. There was also stabling, byre, offices and coachman's house, and a large productive garden. During the 20th century the house was let several times as an unfurnished property. Its end came in 1959 when it was demolished to make way for a housing development. The entrance lodge off Station Road still stands, surrounded by newer houses.

Pretoria Place was erected about 1900 and comprised five shop units at street level with accommodation for thirteen houses above. The corner site at the junction of Station Road and Victoria Place was occupied by chemist John Wood Bennie. The business was later carried on by his widow Mrs Justina Stewart (McKenzie) Bennie until her death in 1945, but has remained as a chemist since then. Its neighbour along Station Road was a confectioner and tearoom and is now the entrance to the pharmacy. The middle portion has been occupied, since 1945, by John Monfries & Sons family grocer and wine merchant who previously had a shop on Main Street, Brightons. The end shops were owned by Redding Co-operative Society and housed grocery and drapery departments. The little building at the end of Pretoria Place was their bakery department, and is now a barber's shop. The Co-operative closed in the early 1970s.

On 18th February 1842 a halt was formed here by the Edinburgh & Glasgow Railway about half a mile to the south of Polmont village. This continued the process of opening up the area that began twenty years earlier with the cutting of the Union Canal, which runs just south of the railway. The line through Falkirk Grahamston made Polmont an important junction and interchange in 1850, a role that increased in 1933 when services to Bo'ness were provided from a bay platform at Polmont until 1956, when Bo'ness Station closed to passengers. The station was extensively modernised in 1984-85 and in 2018 when the Glasgow to Edinburgh railway was electrified.

The Engine Sheds, in a siding south of the line near Polmont Junction, are seen here about 1946. The sheds were built by the North British Railway in 1913-15 to supersede a previous facility at Manuel (Bo'ness Junction) between Polmont and Linlithgow. The locomotives stationed there, 44 in the early 1920s, were mostly used for hauling trains of coal and other minerals. By the late 1950s the sheds were notable because of the number of locomotive classes stabled there, but by that time their utility was in decline, and they closed on 17th May 1964. A marshalling yard north of the sheds took advantage of Polmont's position at a railway junction, acting as the freight interchange.

The Playing Fields, Polmont   No. 4330

This small playground, equipped with the obligatory swings and roundabout, was located at the entrance to St Margaret's Crescent. The photograph was taken around 1954, and features ex-Radio Clyde DJ Bill Smith (standing at the fence on the left) whose postcard collection has been utilised in the compilation of this book. Also in the photograph is his sister Carol who can be seen in the middle of the three girls standing on the right. To the rear of the playing field beside the car were a series of garages for the use of the residents. Today the playground equipment and lock-ups are gone leaving only a fenced off open space in front of St Margaret's House care home.

Some of the post-war non-traditional housing types can be seen at the entrance to St Margaret's Crescent in Polmont, along with the railings of the playground on the left. They include prefabs and flat-roofed steel houses – the first built for speed and the second for cheapness. Alongside the play area is the dark green painted wooden hut run by local councillor William 'Willie' P. Rhind. It sold various grocery items and sweets and as the nearest shops otherwise were on Main Street, was well patronised. Rhind, who represented Redding and Westquarter on Stirling County Council from December 1945 until his death in the autumn of 1969, was honoured with a plaque unveiled in May 1970 in Westquarter School in his memory.

St Margaret's School for Girls in Polmont was a select school founded in 1895 by a company under the patronage of the Duchess of Montrose and 'other well-known ladies and gentlemen'. From 1909 until 1924, it was under the direction of headmistress, Miss Constance Marjory Worsfold assisted (according to an early brochure) by "a large and fully qualified staff of Foreign and English mistresses". Miss Worsfold died in September 1924, and her sister Mrs L. E. Campbell became headmistress. In 1933, following a meeting of parents, former pupils and friends the running of the school was taken over by a new company. The school amalgamated with St Anne's School in Edinburgh, the latter becoming a junior school under the direction of a Miss Jamieson. This company (limited by guarantee), St Margaret's and St Anne's Schools Limited, was set up in such a way as to ensure that no dividends would be payable and that the directors would receive no remuneration for their services. During the Second World War, like many other educational establishments, it temporarily re-located to the countryside, in this instance Muckairn Castle, Taynuilt in Argyll. While the school was based at Taynuilt, their Polmont premises were used by Polish soldiers as a signals training school. The school never returned because the company went into liquidation in June 1947. The buildings were demolished and the stone and fittings sold in October 1948. The site remained empty until the houses on the west side of Stevenson Avenue were built.

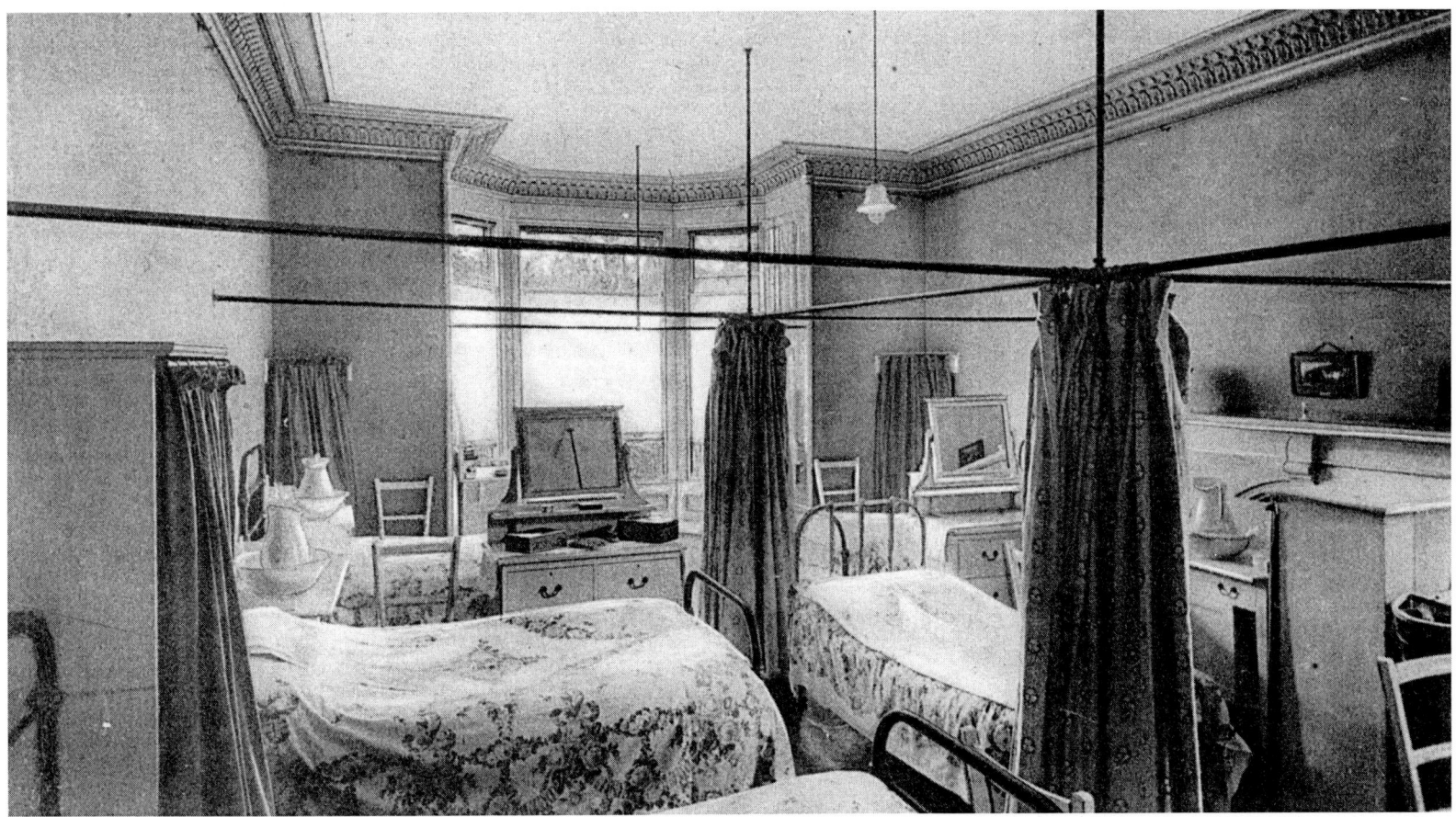

Although day pupils were admitted, St Margaret's School in Polmont was primarily a boarding school drawing their pupils from as far away as Edinburgh and Glasgow. Their two boarding houses, with well appointed dormitories such as the Green Dormitory shown here, could provide accommodation for about 40 pupils. In addition to the dormitories, the school was equipped with a school hall, dining hall, music room, concert room, and a convent. Outdoor recreational facilities were also provided and included a girls garden. Being a 'select' establishment, it was expected that the boarders would make their mark in the world, and, in this respect, they did not lack advice. In July 1933, for example, at the conclusion of a very successful historical pageant, the principal speaker, Lady Whitson cautioned the girls to "consider the vast field that was open to them in the sphere of honorary services in Scotland". In a similar fashion, in July 1939, (prior to their temporary re-location to Taynuilt) the school was addressed by Miss Allison Harvey, President of the Church of Scotland Woman's Guild and a former pupil of the school, who appealed to the girls to become missionaries when they had finished their education. She said that "Scotland led the way in sending out missionaries" and referred to her own work in India.

As well as the provision of a broad based educational curriculum (which included homecraft and first aid), St Margaret's School fully utilised the extensive grounds surrounding the school to also provide a wide range of recreational facilities. In addition to the full size hockey pitch seen here, there were also cricket and lacrosse pitches and two ash tennis courts. A further amenity was a fully enclosed well-stocked garden to enable the girls to 'hone' their gardening skills. In July 1933, as part of their annual speech day, the grounds were put to use to stage an ambitious historical pageant depicting the life of Queen Margaret. The success of this venture – witnessed by a large attendance of parents and relatives – it was stated was in part due to "the picturesque background afforded by the rich foliage of the school policies". Stirlingshire Council intended to build a new school on the playing fields, but it would take until the 1970s before the new St. Margaret's School was built 200 metres further west.

Laurieston looking from the foot of Toll Brae with Grahamsdyke Street running off to the left and Mary Street to the right. The properties seen here are primarily two-storey with either front or rear outside stairs leading to the upper storey. On the extreme right James Street runs parallel to Mary Street past A. & W. Black's Laurieston Church built in 1893. James Street (including the church), and part of Grahamsdyke Street, was cleared for new housing in the early 1960s.

In this view, taken around 1906, the area known locally as the Toll Brae – extending roughly from the Skew Bridge (behind the camera) to Mary Street – is seen prior to the laying down of tramlines. It lay on a direct route east towards the larger Falkirk Burgh, hence the presence of the carriages lined up at the foot of the Brae waiting to take passengers into Falkirk. While in the winter months the Brae would have tasked the horses hauling the carriages up towards Mary Street, it provided rich opportunities for local children – one of whose favourite activities (apart from skating on the nearby Union Canal) was sliding down the Brae. According to one local, "sometimes five or six youngsters would sit on their 'hunkers' with a bigger lad to give them the extra push down the Brae and if the slide got bare more water from the Tommy Will well was put on". All of the old houses that lined the Brae have been demolished.

Falkirk and District tram No. 3 is making its way up the Toll Brae towards the terminus in Mary's Square in Laurieston. The trams were first introduced to Falkirk in October 1905, but it was not until 1909 that a branch line was laid down by Glasgow contractors Messrs A. Stark to serve Laurieston, and this photograph was taken shortly afterwards. In part, the delay was occasioned by the presence of the Skew Bridge (seen in the background). This bridge was constructed to carry the Edinburgh & Glasgow Railway, opened in 1842, over the road but was built obliquely from embankment to embankment hence the name 'skew'. As there was insufficient height, however, the roadway required to be lowered so that the trams could pass under it. The responsibility for excavating the road and laying down the track was met by the tramway company but the re-instatement of the road surface was carried out by the County Council. On 3rd September 1909 two special cars carrying the Transport Manager Douglas Hays and invited guests made their way to the terminus at Laurieston for the official opening ceremony. Although it was always intended to further extend the line east to Polmont, this plan was not followed through and in 1924 the Laurieston route was closed.

Looking north in Mary Square, Laurieston around 1906. The land on the north side of the square was feued in 1762 by Alexander Cowie, a brewer. The buildings on the left comprised two terraced rows of houses – the first with distinctive roof dormer windows was a confectioners shop run by Mrs Neil. The corner property on the right is the Laurieston Co-operative Society's store, selling bakery and drapery items, boots and furniture. The buildings are still owned by the Co-op.

On 2nd April 1910 the area around Mary Square in Laurieston was filled with invited guests to witness Mrs Euphemia Brown, formally open the ornamental gardens. Euphemia was the wife of Charles Brown, factor to the Marquess of Zetland, Lawrence Dundas, whose family named Laurieston. The gardens were the project of Rev A. B. Robb, of Laurieston Church in Mary Street, who gathered support and funds for them. On the north west side of the square a platform was created as a bandstand. The north east and the south west corner, photographed above, had gardens laid out. The north east corner was undeveloped because at the time it was being used to store materials for a construction site nearby, perhaps for the Royal Bar (Tam Bain's) which was being built.

Mary's Square in Laurieston taken c. 1930 looking west. Running across the photograph from left to right is Mary Street with one of Shield's buses and a delivery van. The platform of the bandstand is visible on the right with a lamp in its centre provided by the Polmont Gas Company. J. Moffat now occupies Mclaren Bros former premises. The gardens laid out in 1910 are now just a simple flower bed surrounded by turf.

This late 1920s view of the north east corner of Mary's Square in Laurieston is dominated by a two-storey building with ogee-domed octagonal corner turret. It was built in 1910 in the Jacobean Renaissance style, and externally at least, is largely unchanged. Largely unchanged too is the attached two storey building to the left of the main building. The little row of cottages have been replaced by a single-storey extension to the public house and a modern development. Most of the ground floor of the 1910 building is occupied by the Royal Bar one of Laurieston's most iconic public houses, made even more so when, in 1955, it changed to its present name of Tam Bain's. The Tam in question (also known as the 'Lum Man') was a local man of property who had a house in the Square but who fell out with the town's feuars when they objected to his plan to add an outside stair to his house. In retaliation, Tam commissioned John Morrison a local stone mason to construct a chimney lum (pot) in his image which he promptly fixed to the roof of his house. In 1955 the lost chimney pot was recovered and placed in a glass case within the public house where it remains to this day. Local folklore suggests an alternative version, that it was sculpted in the shape of a man and attached to the roof of a house in the square by a husband to taunt his wife who refused to allow him to smoke at home. Next to the pub, in the square, is a K1 style telephone box, introduced in 1921, although the long windows are a design that dates from 1927. The K1 was made from three slabs of concrete and a wooden door and topped by a pyramid roof finished with ornate ironwork. Laurieston War Memorial, on the right was designed by sculptor William C. Roberts. This 22 feet high Creetown granite Celtic Cross was unveiled by Major Glyn MP on 27th August 1921.

Laurieston School.

The former Laurieston School, built in 1876, seen here around 1918, was situated at the junction of Boyd Street and School Road. In 1969 it was replaced by a new school situated just to the east, but still conveniently on School Road. Prior to the establishment of the Board School there were several schools in Laurieston including a private school taught by William Bryce and Mr Hardie's school in the Square. The "Auld School" in the square was also used for all sorts of other community activities and meetings. In June 1934, the Square was the scene of much pomp and pageantry when during a 'Children's Carnival' the 'Queen' for the day, twelve year old Hazel Harvey, a pupil of the local school, deposited a bouquet of flowers at the base of the War Memorial. The Carnival attracted an estimated 8,000 spectators.

On 4th December 1913 a public meeting was held in Laurieston School to consider the establishment of a bowling club. After much discussion regarding possible sites, it was decided to lay down a green to the north of Polmont Road. To raise funds for their new venture, a grand Jumble Sale was held in the Century Hall on Saturday 28th March 1915 that included air gun and wall quoits competitions. Later that year a three-day bazaar was held in Falkirk Town Hall. Although possible sites for the green were identified, negotiations ceased on the outbreak of the First World War and it was not until 1919 that the matter was again considered. One possibility was to the 'north side of Grahamsdyke Road' but this was considered too expensive and 'unfit for purpose' because of underground workings. Another, situated on the part of Polmont Road called Victoria Road, was 'deemed then best'. On 23rd July 1920 a public meeting was held in the Old School Room to propose the constitution and 29 members signed up paying an annual fee of 2s 6d each. On 28th June 1923 the green was officially opened along with the first clubhouse. In this photo, framed by some of the houses that line Polmont Road, several matches are in progress. Just in picture on the right is the old tennis court pavilion which has since been replaced.

The 'model' village at Westquarter near Polmont – part of which is seen here – was built by Stirlingshire County Council in the grounds of Westquarter estate principally to house residents of sub-standard miners' rows at Standburn and neighbouring villages. Until 1912 Westquarter House was the property of coal master James Nimmo whose company worked several pits locally. For the following eight years Glasgow merchant Cyril Herbert Dunderdale owned the estate. The house was let out to other tenants until 1934 when it was bought by Stirlingshire County Council and demolished (including lodge and doocot) to enable the building of the 'model' village. This was designed by architect John A. W. Grant FRIAS, Edinburgh in the arts and crafts style and built between 1935 and 1938. The cost of around 450 houses to accommodate almost 3,000 persons at Westquarter was approximately £193,000. The development was not wholly welcomed by its intended residents, many of whom were unemployed because of pit closures and were concerned that higher rents would make it harder to afford fares for travel to work. Rents in the new houses were typically 6s 9d a week for 3-bedroom apartments as opposed to 2s 6d for a single room and kitchen or 3s 6d for a double roomed house at Standburn.

Shortly after this photograph was taken in 1929, all of the buildings seen here in Main Street, Redding were pulled down to be replaced with council housing. The most prominent of these properties was the two-storey Abercrombie Buildings which housed a sub-post office and newsagent and confectioners shop then operated by postmistress Jean Burleigh. Main Street (also known variously as School Road or Back Road) was a busy thoroughfare. An Austin 7 Box Saloon sits outside the post office, a coal lorry and a horse-drawn delivery van are plying their trade further up the street.

This typical miners 'row' which stood on the north west arm of Redding Cross is a reminder of the importance of coal mining in the area. The Redding Pit, operated by coal masters James Nimmo & Company, was the largest in the Falkirk district and contributed to the growing population of Redding village which had reached 600 by the 1850s. Many of the miners were accommodated in 'rows' such as the one seen here with amenities which can only be described as basic. Water, for example, for washing and cooking was taken from standpipes supplemented by rain water channelled via rones into the water butts outside the doors of each cottage. Hot water for baths, which typically took the form of zinc or wooden tubs on the kitchen floor, was supplied from coal-fired copper boilers. Education for the children of the Redding miners, likewise, was often rudimentary being provided from 1875-1910 in a colliery schoolroom in nearby Reddingmuirhead. Inevitably, the living and working conditions of the miners resulted in the establishment of numerous trade union lodges formed to fight for better conditions. The first of these lodges, the Sir Wm Wallace Grand Lodge of Scotland Free Colliers, was established in Redding village in 1863, and, despite the closure of all of the local coal mines, continues today.

In this photograph of Redding Cross taken in June 1928, the miners' row on the facing page is on the left and the north east arm of the cross heads into the distance along Main Street. The rows were demolished in the early 1930s and the site has remained open space ever since. The memorial to the Redding Pit Disaster was placed there in 1980. To the right of photograph is the Crossroads Inn with more shops further along. The shops fell victim to a road widening scheme in 1930, leaving only the Crossroads Inn standing which itself was cleared in the 1970s to improve the junction. Behind the inn, where the houses of Waverley Park are now, was a wooden hall that was used for billiards. Its owner was a regular at Falkirk Sheriff Court receiving fines for allowing betting to take place on the premises. Betting shops became legal on 1st January 1961, and soon after the billiard hall started operating one.

Prior to the provision of a new school for Redding (seen here around 1904), the village had to make do with a small one-storey school described in an *Ordnance Survey Notebook* as "where an average of sixty scholars were taught the ordinary branches". Lacking government allowances and endowments, the master's total fees amounted to £46 a year. In 1900 there were a series of meetings on improving Redding's school accommodation and it was decided that building a new school was preferable to enlarging the existing building. A new site was chosen on Redding Road where Grange Place is now. The new school opened 11th May 1903 and was demolished in the 1970s. In 1923 the staff raised £18 12s 6d for the Central Relief Fund in aid of sufferers of the Redding Pit Disaster. The old school was used for worship but this was considered unsatisfactory by the Presbytery of Linlithgow, as the Moderator reported to the Kirk Session in April 1902 that the question of a meeting place or mission church at Redding had been discussed by the Presbytery. It would take until 15th June 1907 before the Mission Church was opened on the old quoiting ground, where it still stands as Laurieston, Redding and Westquarter Parish Church.

The No 23 Pit at Redding seen here alongside the Union Canal, was one of several owned by James Nimmo and Company and is chiefly remembered for the terrible tragedy that resulted in the loss of 40 men on 25th September 1923. There had been many pits in the Redding area, and because of this there were extensive abandoned underground workings in the area. At the time of the accident No. 23 Pit was removing coal along a geological fault, which was believed to be a sufficient barrier to water in flooded mine workings on the other side. Unknown to the mine engineers, because it was unmarked on the plans of the abandoned mine, there was a sump cut into the faulted rock. This thinner section gave way and water flooded into No. 23 Pit. There were 72 miners working on the night shift. Six escaped during the initial flood but 66 were trapped underground. After five hours 21 men were rescued through an old air shaft. The mine's own pumps, supplemented by equipment from other collieries, began pumping the water into the Union Canal and a team of divers was brought in to search the flooded sections. Nine days after the inrush, as pumping efforts lowered the water in the mine, five more men were rescued; they would be the last. A Central Relief Fund established in aid of sufferers of the Redding Pit Disaster raised some £22,000. The donations came from many sources and included £55 10s from the Head Office and local branches of the British Linen Bank, £18 12s 6d from the staff of Redding Public School and £14 19s 4d from Muiravonside Parish Church. A sum of £52 was donated by the Scottish General Omnibus Company Limited and the Falkirk and District Tramways which was later augmented by the sum of £226 from the sale of special tickets on the tramway and omnibus routes. The last body was recovered on 3rd December 1923, and in January the following year the pit reopened. In May 1958 the pit was closed by the National Coal Board.

Of all the local educational establishments, Blairlodge Academy (located to the south of Redding village alongside the Union Canal) was the most prestigious and seen here c. 1905. John Johnston inherited the land at Blairs in 1822 and before his death in 1841 had Blairlodge House constructed as a Georgian style villa replacing an earlier house. In 1843 Reverend Robert Cunningham bought the house with the intention of using it to form the nucleus for a very select boarding school. He was headmaster of the school until 1851 when he took on Robert Hislop as a partner, after which he slowly withdrew from running the school. It particularly flourished under the dynamic headmaster, J. Cooke Gray, who took over the Academy in 1874. To cater for the increasing numbers of boarders an annexe (seen here to the right of photograph) was erected in 1888. In June 1891 the Academy was advertising for pupils for their junior school, Meadowbank House, that took pupils between the ages of 7 and 12 years for an annual fee of 80 guineas. In 1894 the school (under the Inspection and Examination of the Scotch Education Department for Higher-Class Schools) advertised that reports stated "it is one of the marvels of Private Enterprise and a model of what every High-Class Public School ought nowadays to be". Shortly after Cooke Gray's death in 1902, however, financial difficulties together with a particularly virulent measles epidemic, brought about the demise of the school. In March 1905 the academy was offered for sale, advertised as recently carried out as a high class school for boys with accommodation for 200+ boarders; equipped with laboratories, workshops, gymnasium, cricket pavilion, hospital, stable byre etc. It would take six years before it was sold for use as a borstal.

Prison officers outside Polmont Young Offenders Institution in 1914. In March 1911 the former Blairlodge School buildings and land were acquired by the HM Prison Commissioners for Scotland for adaptation as a Young Offenders Institution and shortly afterwards, on 1st October 1911, was opened as Scotland's first borstal. The first governor appointed by the Secretary for Scotland was Captain Raymond Pelly Houston Monro, the then deputy governor of Barlinnie Prison. Shocked by the news, 'old boys' of the school petitioned not to have the Blairlodge name used and the establishment became Polmont Institution. It was substantially rebuilt in 2005 and the original mansion house was demolished in 2010.

In this view, taken in June 1928, the camera is pointing along Shieldhill's Main Street and its junction with Crossbrae is just behind the photographer. From left to right are the Shieldhill Miners Welfare Hall, the 26 feet high granite obelisk of the village war memorial (partially hidden by a hedge) and the Muiravon Free Church with its protruding front gable and, finally, the terraced miners cottages known locally as the 'Top Row'. The first named was built at a cost of £2,150 and was the 80th Welfare Hall funded by the Central Welfare Committee for the Lanarkshire mining area. When completed, comprised a hall capable of accommodating 250 people, two ante-rooms, a cinematograph operating chamber and a spacious billiard room with two full-sized tables. It was officially opened in September 1925 by the welfare supervisor for the Lanarkshire area, R. J. Prince. As it was (apart from the hall within the local school) the only sizeable public space in the village, it was much used for socials, dances, plays, cantatas and film shows. Today, the Welfare Hall functions as a community hall. The war memorial (strictly speaking the Easter and Wester Shieldhill and Simmerhouses War Memorial) was built on land gifted by John McIsaac of Greenmount Farm and commemorates the 20 men of Easter and Wester Shieldhill and Simmerhouses who lost their lives in the Great War. Constructed at a cost of £350 it was unveiled 1st June 1924 by Captain Thomas Harvey of Weedingshall.

In this photograph (taken around 1910) the occupants are pictured outside the row of stone-built cottages known locally as 'The Cyclist's Rest' in Herdshill. It was aptly named as it stood high on the moors above Falkirk. Thirsty cyclists were perhaps served by the small general store forming part of the ground floor end cottage with the dormer window. Clearly an entrepreneur, its owner, Mrs Gordon, also rented out the upper floor to the village school teachers. The shop was later taken over by Toby Hunter who expanded its business to become a grocer and a fish and chip shop. Just visible to the right of photograph is the roof of a detached cottage alongside the row which contained a butcher's shop owned by Willie Hunter which had a slaughter house on the lower level. Cattle, driven straight from the market on the hoof, provided the supply of beef for the shop (where Mrs Hunter served), while Willie sold the produce from a van in the local area. The cottages nearest the camera and the one with the dormer windows still stand opposite Anderson Crescent in Shieldhill.

In this late 1950s scene several traders (including a Brown Brothers Limited, Edinburgh, van) can be seen on the Redding Road near Brightons Cross. Apart fom the Trustee Savings Bank, opened by the Falkirk Savings Bank in 1914, all of the other dwellings are houses. Just out of picture on the right was the Brightons Picture House which was opened 23rd December 1914 to music and "a First-Class programme of pictures" and lasted until about 1961 when it was converted to a bingo hall. Note the 1950s Austin A30 and the 1940s Foder lorry further down Redding Road and the 1940s Hillman Minx next to the bank.

In this view, the portion of the Albert Place buildings that front Maddiston Road are on the left. Although the road itself has since been paved and widened, remarkably there has been little change with many of the buildings lining the right side of the street remaining. On the junction of Maddiston Road and Waggon Road proper, the building alongside the man and children is now the Brightons Inn. A little further up, the tallish two-storey building beyond the dormer-roofed properties is presently Lodge Polmont No 793 Masonic Hall. This lodge first met on Wednesday 20th September 1893, in the upper floor of Glenedge Cottage in nearby Quarry Brae, which was known locally as 'The Lodge in the Garret'. Weekly meetings were held until the consecration of the lodge on 18th October 1893 by Bro George Christie, Right Worshipful Provincial Grand Master of Stirlingshire. The laying of the foundation stone of the new Lodge took place on 8th June 1895, and the new premises were consecrated by Christie on 20th November that year.

Albert Place at the Cross Brightons in June 1928. Externally, apart from the arched doorway between the two cars, this building is unchanged. George Simpson, who died in September 1941, lived above his shop and was a well-respected member of the local community. In addition to serving on the old Grangemouth School Board and, later, the local School Management Board, he was a JP (elected in 1930) and served on Stirlingshire County Council representing Muiravonside West from 1926 until 1938. To his right on Maddiston Road alongside the 1926 Morris Cowley Bullnose car are motor agents O. A. Goodfellow, and behind the 1920s Morris Snubnose van is A. & J. Paterson's grocers and general merchants shop which was active in the early 1930s.

A 1920s view of Albert Place looking along Main Street and Maddiston Road (right of photograph). The only casualty of later redevelopment is the single-storey property between the Albert Place building and the cottages with roof dormers, which have since gone leaving a gap site.

MAIN STREET AND U.F. CHURCH, BRIGHTONS, POLMONT

Late 19th century semi-detached houses on the north side of Main Street between present day Randolph Crescent and Brightons Cross. These are largely unchanged today. On the opposite side of Main Street is the steeple of Brightons Parish Church. It started life as a Free Church and was built between 1846 and 1847 by Glasgow architects Brown & Carrick using stone from a nearby quarry gifted by the quarry owner Alexander Lawrie (who also gifted the land). T-plan side galleries were added in 1893. In 1929 the United Free Church merged with the Church of Scotland and it became Polmont South Parish Church.

Drumbowie Public School was replaced in 1976 by the present day school following a long local campaign against closure. By all accounts, Standburn's annual Drumbowie Public School Children's Gala was the highlight of the year. Prior to Gala Day, the miners' wives sewed the costumes for the historical pageant while their husbands constructed wooden arches for erection throughout the village. To brighten up the place, window shutters and doors were painted and pavement kerbs whitened. Alongside each of the six miners' rows, banners and bunting was erected. The highlight of the day was the parade itself. By tradition it would be headed by a band that would be expected to play throughout their one mile walk from Bowhouse Station and especially loudly when entering the village at the 'top of the gullet'. The assembly point was within the school playground and thereafter the parade, headed by a pupil on horseback, would make their way down Main Street and round the 'rows' towards Fairview Park for refreshments and an afternoon of games. After the sports, many of the adults would repair to the Gothenburg public house locally known as 'the squech' before later putting on their best 'togs' for the Gala Day Dance in the Miners' Welfare Hall.

Muiravonside Parish Church and churchyard, seen here around 1913, was built in 1806 on the foundations of an earlier church described as 'old' in 1791. It is a barn like church with tall pointed windows lying beside the Union Canal. The windows contain stained glass depicting the ministry of Rev. George Keith at Muiravonside from 1871 to 1884. The belfry predates the church, and its bell has the inscription 'FOR THE KIRK OF MUIRAVONSIDE IOHN MEIKLE ME FECIT/EDINBIRGI 1699' (*Me Fecit* – I made it), and both likely came from the earlier church. A horseshoe gallery surrounded the 'preaching kirk' pulpit until 1947, when the church was found to be badly affected by woodworm and dry rot necessitating a complete internal renovation. The replanned interior includes an aisle running from the east to a pulpit at the west gable. Since 2008 it has been linked with the nearby Blackbraes and Shieldhill Church. Running alongside the church is the 30 mile long Union Canal which was built by engineer Hugh Baird to connect Edinburgh and Falkirk. It opened in 1822 and carried materials for the rapidly developing New Town of Edinburgh. It flourished for nearly 20 years until the Edinburgh & Glasgow Railway was completed in 1842. The canal lost all its passenger traffic and time-sensitive cargoes to the railway, which bought the canal in 1849. It closed to commercial traffic in 1933 and formally closed in 1965. For the following decades it lay abandoned, slowly decaying until it was restored and reopened in 2002.